My Big Christmas Coloring Book

BuzzPop

Merry Christmas, friends!

The bear lost a boot! Connect the dots to keep his foot dry.

Time to decorate the Christmas tree!

Here's a big star for the top of the tree!
How many points does it have? Count them and write down the number.
Then color the star any way you wish.

Answer: _____

Santa needs help finding your present.
Decorate this box so that he knows it's for you.

Welcome to Candy Cane Lane!

Circle your favorite cookie.

Decorate this gingerbread house.
Draw your favorite candies all over it!

Circle the two matching gingerbread cookies.

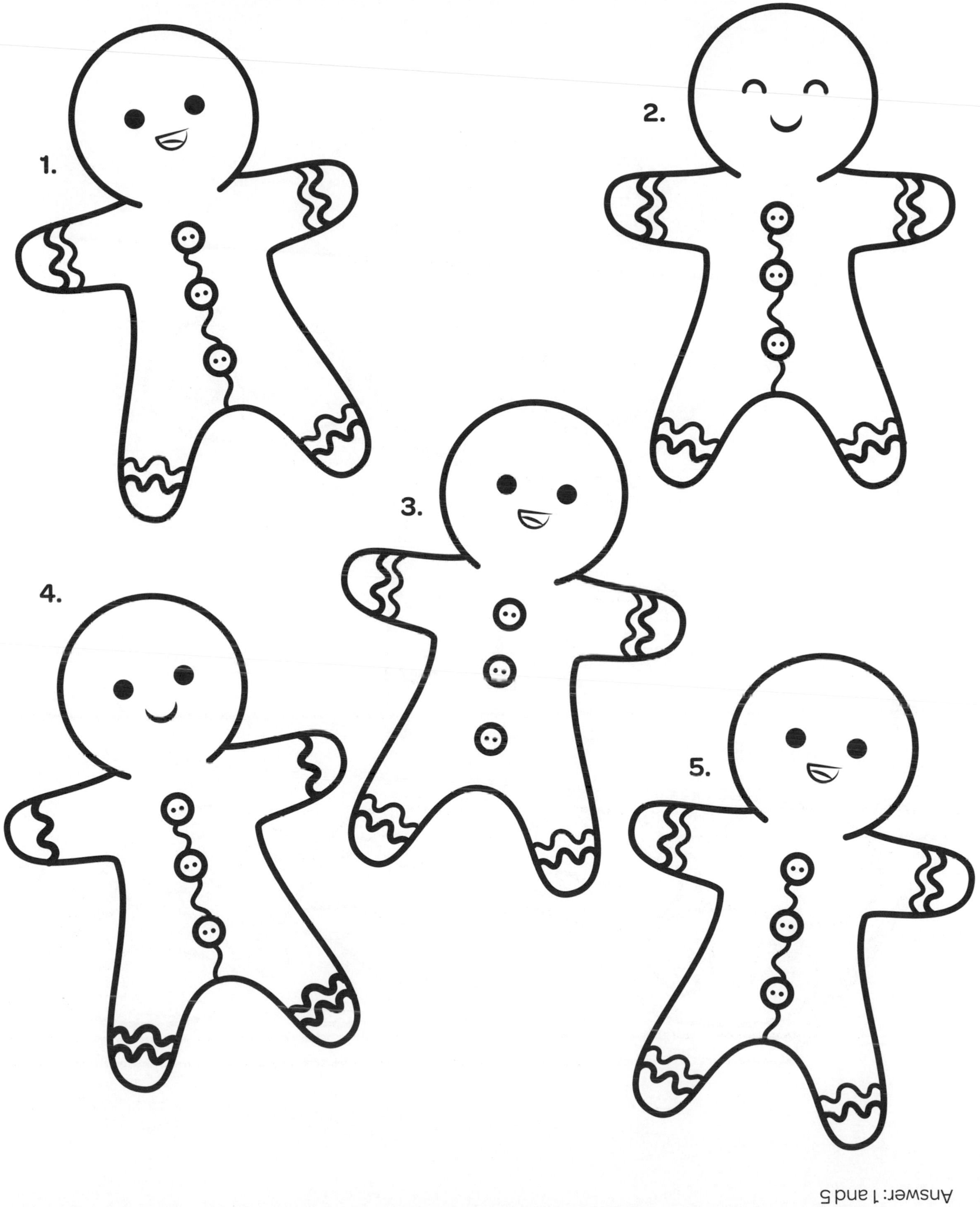

Answer: 1 and 5

Yummy rolls for Christmas dinner!

This Christmas cake is called a buche de noel.

The family is enjoying a holiday by the fireplace.

What colors can you add to this pretty snowflake?

Unscramble the word to finish the message.

WE ARE GOING TO BUILD A NOMSWAN

_ _ _ _ _ _ _

Which snowplow will go to the house?

FINISH

Kittens love boxes and ribbons!

Bundle up for the cold weather!

Is every snowflake different?
Circle the two that match.

What comes next in each frosty pattern?

1.

2.

3.

4.

Learn to draw a snowflake.

Draw one here:

How many snowballs does this otter have?

Answer: _____

Jack Frost likes to make patterns on windows.

**Draw two more patterns on the blank windows.
Then color the patterns any way you wish.**

Ice-skating is such fun.

He can make a figure eight!

Here comes the snowplow!

A sled is flat and goes down hills fast.

A sleigh has runners, which look like skis.
They need animals to pull them through the snow.

Let's play outside! Connect the dots to see what you need to wear.

**Unscramble the names
of these winter words:**

LICCIE

_ _ _ _ _ _

TISENTM

_ _ _ _ _ _ _

OBOST

_ _ _ _ _

Christmas sweaters are cozy!

Complete the pattern on this cozy sweater-vest!

Don't forget your boots!

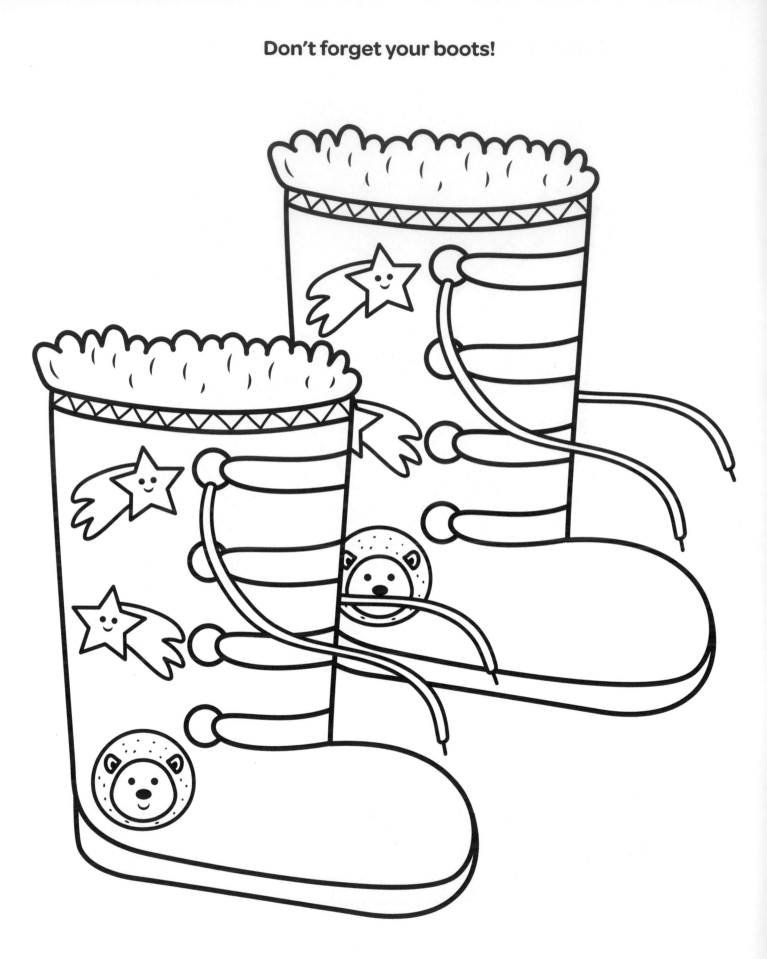

Find and circle the four items you will need in cold weather.

Add holiday clothing to the foxes to help them stay warm!

There's a message for you!
Use this code to find out what it says.

= A

= E

= H

= I

= L

= N

= 0

= P

= S

= T

= V

= W

= Y

This kitten likes to catch the
snowflakes before they melt.

Warm socks for toasty toes!

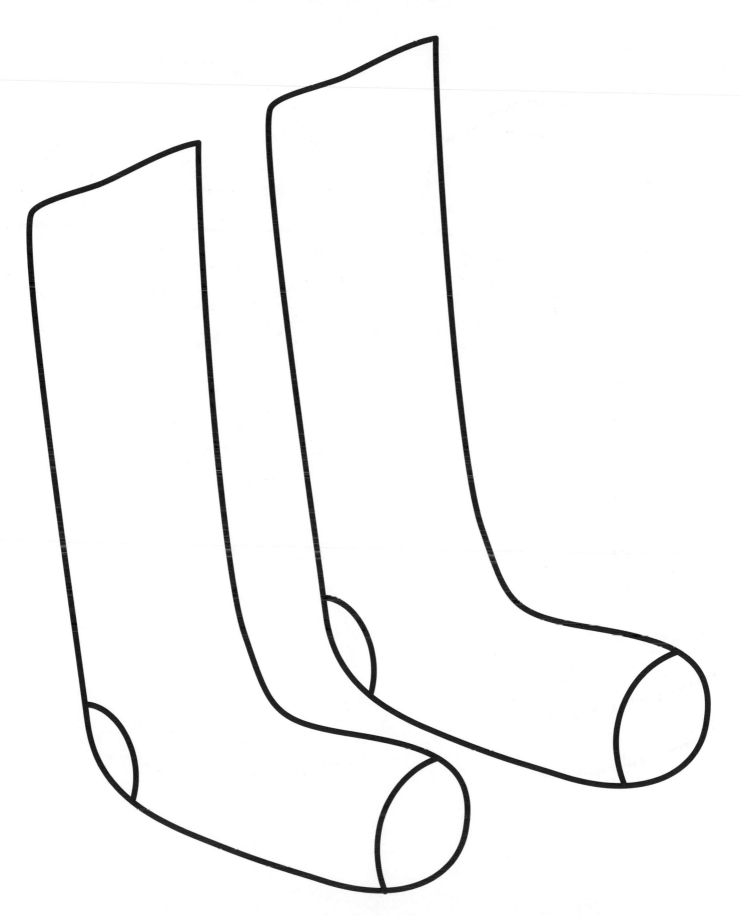

Wonderful, warm, winter hats!

Create a pattern on this Christmas sweater.

What a pretty Christmas wreath!

Toy stores are full of holiday fun.

The city is pretty under the northern lights!

Let's have a feast!

Most dragons breathe fire. What does an ice dragon breathe?

The Snow Queen likes to spread frost wherever she goes.

The seal and penguin are having a picnic.

This penguin likes to swim with the fish.

The king is ready for his Christmas banquet.
Add two cupcakes and three glasses of juice
to the table.

Soup warms us up on cold days!

Time for a Christmas tale!

What is on TV on Christmas Eve?

We make ornaments with pinecones.

How many marshmallows are in our mugs of hot chocolate?

Answer: _____

Circle the two matching quilts.

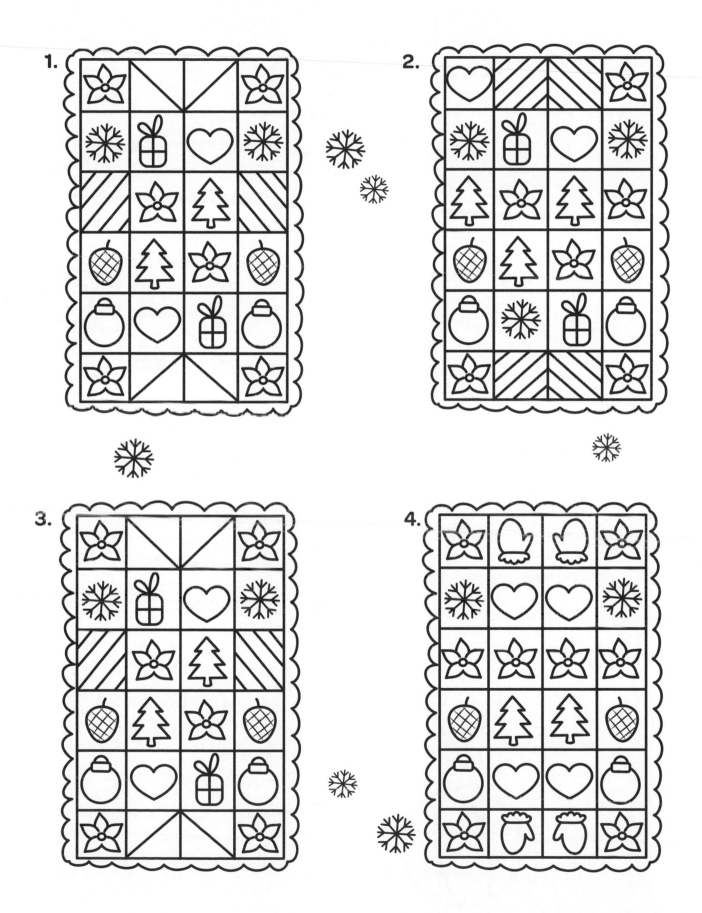

Let's hide in our blanket fort!

This snowman needs help being built.
Look at the objects below and draw them in the correct order on the right-hand page. He will be so happy you helped!

**Connect the dots to find the snowman.
Then, give him a colorful hat and scarf.**

You can go fishing even at Christmas!

Time to ski down the slope!

What a cool scarf!

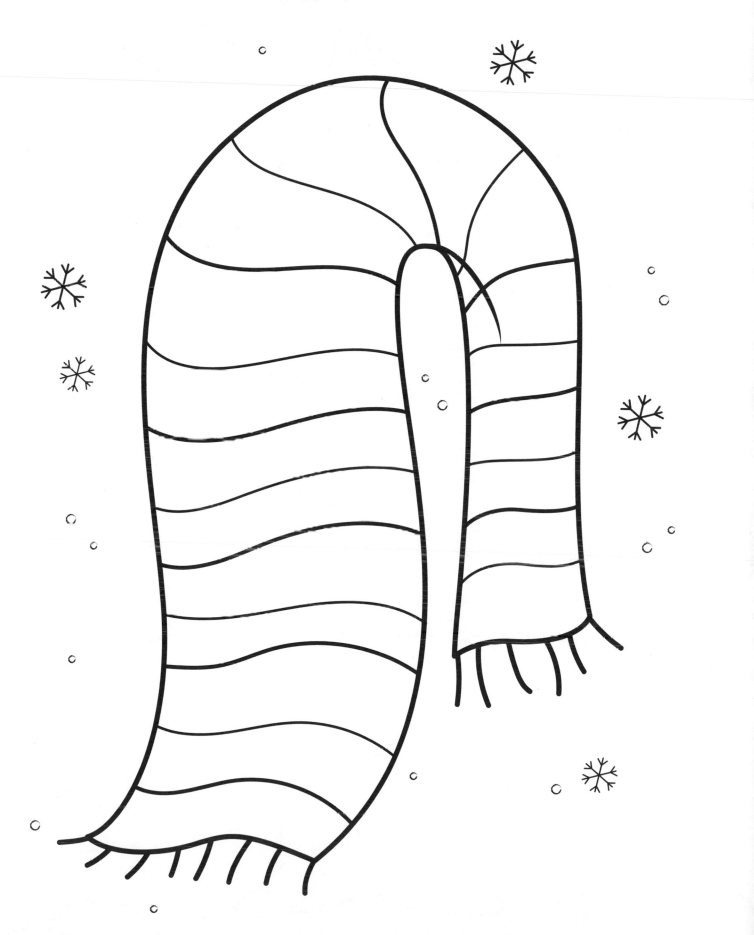

Look at all the pretty patterns this girl is wearing on her outfit!

Hanukkah is here. We use the middle candle to light the others on the menorah!

It's time to play a Hanukkah game. Let's spin the dreidel!

How many pieces of gelt did you receive?

Write the total here: _____

We love to eat latkes on Hanukkah. They are potato pancakes!

Students can't wait for winter break!

Christmas is a time for giving!

Decorate the Christmas tree!

Learn to draw a penguin.

Draw one here:

Christmas oranges are a sweet treat!

Snacks for Santa.

We share breakfast on Christmas morning!

We like to sing Christmas carols.

Who pulls Santa's sleigh?

Pick the correct path to help these explorers find the North Pole!

START

A.

B.

C.

FINISH

Answer: B

Learn to draw Santa Claus.

1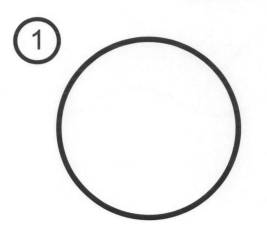

2

3

4

5

Draw him here:

Santa is in his workshop!

The elves have made lots of toys for Santa's bag.

Wrapping presents is so much fun!

Christmas treats are fun to give!

Help the reindeer guide Santa to your house.
Pick the correct path for them to follow!

START

A.

B.

C.

FINISH

Answer: C

**Everyone is celebrating together!
Color in Santa and his friends.**

**Christmas stockings are ready for
Santa to fill with presents!**

This Advent wreath helps us count down to Christmas.

We leave treats for Santa and his reindeer on Christmas Eve.

Did you get what you wished for? Draw a gift here.

Kwanzaa has three colors connected to the holiday.
Color the flag by the numbers:
1 – red; 2 – black; 3 – green

The kinara holds seven candles, one for each principle of Kwanzaa.
Color the candles by the numbers:
1 – red; 2 – black; 3 – green

We celebrate a good harvest at Kwanzaa.

The Kikombe Cha Umoja is
also known as the Unity Cup!

Kwanzaa is a time for gifts! Draw your present on the table.

**Candles are an important part of many holiday traditions.
Match the candles to their holidays.**

1. CHRISTMAS

A.

2. KWANZAA

B.

3. HANUKKAH

C.

Match the winter words to their pictures.

1. SNOWFLAKE

2. SCARF

3. SHOVEL

4. MUG

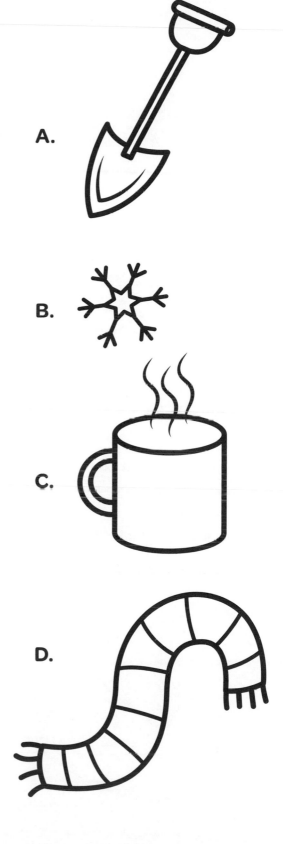

A.

B.

C.

D.

The clock strikes midnight on New Year's Eve!

Let's wear fancy hats.

What is this walrus wearing on its head?

Everyone loves to celebrate together!

When it gets really cold, it means
Old Man Winter is ready to visit us.
Which path will he use to find the houses?

START

A.

B.

C.

FINISH

Go to sleep so that Santa can visit!

Not a creature was stirring,
except for this lucky mouse!

Holly, jolly Christmas tree ornaments!

A bird for our Christmas tree!

A reindeer ornament is cute as can be.

Vikings send yuletide greetings!

Sailors send season's greetings!

Who's going to the forest?

START

B.

A.

FINISH

The North Wind is fierce and strong.

In Australia, Christmas is in the summer.

How many owls can you find in the forest?

Answer: _____

Can you decode this message?
What does it say about the weather?

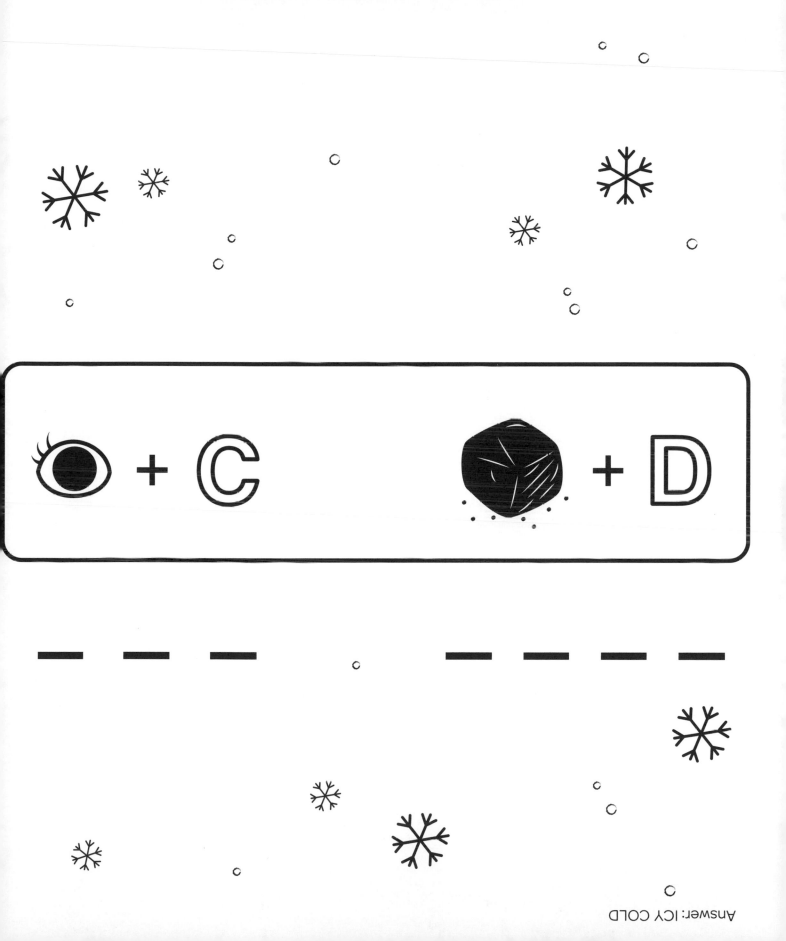

Learn to draw an ice fairy.

Draw her here:

The king shares his Christmas meal.

Look at the fireworks for the new year!

Geese need to fly south for the winter.
Which goose is going toward sunny weather?

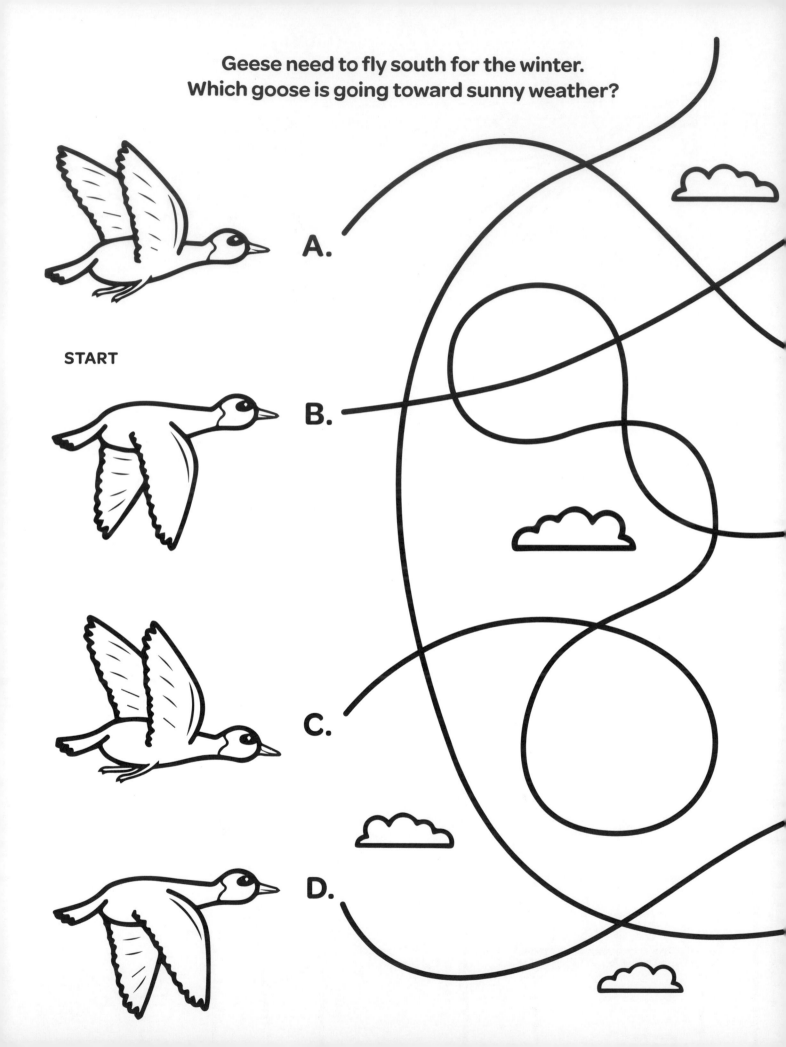

A.

START

B.

C.

D.

FINISH

Look at all the treats for our festive hot pot on New Year's.

Design your own snowflake pattern.

This is no bear—it's a woolly bear caterpillar, and it loves the cold.

Canned and pickled veggies are a tasty winter snack!

It's time to make a Christmas stew.

Sharing is caring during the holidays!

We have fun indoors on cold days!

We play hockey in the winter!

Say hello to the narwhals.

Can you make a festive wreath?

Snowball fight!

We like watching movies during the holidays.

Add your favorite movie to the screen.

Wool keeps us warm!

Smitten by mittens.

Match the words to the pictures!

1. MOOSE

A.

2. HAT

B.

3. PENGUIN

C.

Learn to draw a log cabin.

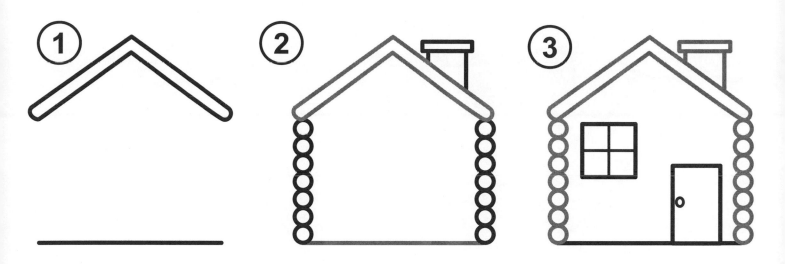

Draw it here:

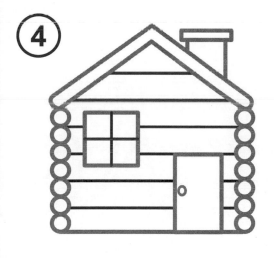

After hiking, we like to have a winter picnic.

Connect the dots on this tent so that we can sleep tight!

8

9

10

11

12

13

14

Pick the correct path to get to the Christmas cabin.

FINISH

How many penguins are at the zoo?
Write your answer here: _____

Answer: 7

These houses are ready for the holidays!

Design your own snowflake!

This house is covered in icicles.

Time for bed on this Christmas Eve.